Dedicated to

all those who live

In the land of Imagination

and Infinite Possibilities

Credits

Publisher: Vaishali and Elliot Malach, Purple Haze Press™
Executive Producer Rangel: Elliot Malach
Purr Production – Bliss & Grace
Big G – The Big Bang Boss

Project Director/Editor: Bethany Argisle, Argisle Enterprises Inc.

Book Design, Layout and Cover Jacket Design: Albert Howell, Meta4 Productions

Cover Art and Illustrations: Brian Narelle, Narelle Creative

Marie Loverich: Illustrations

Editorial Staff: Orion Torney, Jessica Brunner

First Printing, April 2006.

Library of Congress Cataloging in Public Data

Vaishali, 1959 -

It's Time To Wake Up with the You Are What You Love Playbook

ISBN 0-9773200-1-4

1. Love 2. Self-Help 3. Spirituality 4. Consciousness Education

Table of Contents

PLAYBOOK

Introduction

There is only the One, there is always infinite abundance

These days, most books come with a companion workbook. The greatest learning experiences, I have found, came while in a playful mindset. Play is expansive. Play is healing. Play is creative. Play is spontaneous. Play is an activity of the Heart, not the head. Most of all play is fun. Play is about being in the present moment and not having a problem with it. Play is about remembering not to take life to seriously, because we do not know what reality is. Play is a world of unlimited imagination and infinite possibility. Play is simply the best of all possible teachers.

In my lifetime, I have been diagnosed not once, but twice as terminal. I have lived through mind-bending, off the charts, experiences of physical pain from both illness, as well as injury. I have suffered the emotional and psychological minefield of betrayal and abuse. I have lived through the American right of passage known as divorce. I have survived unfair and unjust legal trials. I have been cheated on, lied to, ripped off and abandoned by the very people who were supposed to have loved me the most; and through it all I have learned that indeed laughing at disaster is the best medicine. I have made Bugs Bunny my official religious symbol to which I give homage and respect on a regular basis.

Bugs has taught me everything I need to know about how to live a successful life. Bugs has mastered a mindset that is untouchable and incorruptible by anything in the physical, temporal world. Bugs reminds me that I do not know what reality is, so relax and enjoy the ride. Bugs embodies an amazing life of flexibility, as well as resilience. In my next life I hope to come back as Bugs Bunny! I cannot imagine a more exalted or fulfilled existence, or better royalties.

In the name of all that is Holy, Sacred and Bugs Bunny, I could not inflict something on you called a workbook. I bless you with a healing, rejuvenating gift known as a playbook. This book is designed to increase your experience of life, as a playful arena in which we are invited to humanifest the loving, happy world of our highest, most fulfilling dreams. The intention of this playbook is to beckon you into a more accepting, playful, lighthearted adventure through the power of awareness.

The book is meant to be a springboard of creative suggestions. Please feel free to be limited only by your imagination and sense of creative playfulness. Remember you cannot be playful and worried at the same time. You cannot be childlike and uptight at the same time. You cannot be creative and be re-creating your old patterns at the same time. Therefore creative playfulness is its own reward. Be happy! Be healthy! Most of all be successfully playful in everything you give your attention to. May we all play as one!

Humanifest the loving, happy world of our
highest, most fulfilling dreams

PLAYBOOK

Playing in the Dreamland

There to be the One, where is always infinite abundance

I adore dreamtime. One might even say, **I live to dream, and dream to live.** Dreamtime is a remarkably flexible reality. Anything and everything is possible in the dream world. Everyone has experienced having a dream that they never wanted to wake up from. And everyone has experienced a dream we could not wake up from fast enough. Yet, for all its wide range of emotional potential, dreamtime is still the most incredibly information rich environment. Everything you ever wanted to know from the "know thyself" quest is offered to each of us in dreamtime. In this section, we look at tips for lucid as well as non-lucid dreaming.

Let's start with non-lucid or regular dreaming. The best dream preparation always happens in waking reality. Writing down or reviewing in your mind what information you would like in a dream is one of the best techniques. Imagine you are working on some relationship dilemma and you would like more feedback from the whole of your mind. Ask for the answer in a dream. Spend time during your waking reality getting clear about exactly what the issue is, and what questions you would like more commentary on. Spending time incubating a question for a future dream response is always a well-rewarded practice. In addition to that, I find spending time, thirty minutes to an hour just before bedtime, refining the process of asking for clarity, is highly efficient.

Reviewing the issue and then writing down the questions and difficulties to resolving a problem, always pushes the information deeper through the nervous system. This helps to plant the dream seed. Then as you are falling asleep, hold the intention that you will receive the needed information requested in your dreams. Continue to repeat the affirmation and intention that you will have a dream, revealing what you need to know.

Keep the written questions next to your bed with a pen or pencil or tape deck. If you should awaken, write down anything you remember. As you return to sleep again maintain the intention that your dreams will deliver the answers you are looking for. Upon waking, it is essential at that time you write down whatever impressions or details you remember, even if it is just a feeling.

Remembering dream information is a practice you coordinate with the rest of your mind. Think of remembering your dreams as a relationship similar to a pitcher and a catcher in a baseball game. The pitcher is not going to pitch the ball until the catcher is in the proper position. Dreaming is self-communication at its finest. If you are not going to listen to your information, you won't pitch yourself the dream ball. You may be able to fool others in life, but it is infinitely harder to fool yourself. Practice telling yourself that you will remember your dreams upon awakening. Every time you wake up, practice writing down every detail. Before you know it, you will be pitching yourself more and more dream-motivational information. You may start out the first time waking up and writing down only a few words. However, by the end of a week or two you will find you have pages of information streaming out of you.

Holding intention is critical in either lucid or non-lucid dreaming. Ask for the specific information that you want. Then hold the intention that you will remember the information when it is given. There are really no short cuts in the process. It is all about practice. The more frequently you practice holding these intentions, the more confident and skilled you will become.

Interpretation is a lot trickier than remembering or incubating a dream question. I find that most books offering a guided interpretation on symbols and images are limited at best. The reason for this is due to the fact that images and symbols can change in meaning over time. For example you may have a dream about traveling somewhere; one time you have the dream, traveling may represent the need to visit parts of the mind unfamiliar to you; the next time you have a dream the traveling may be a commentary on how creating a new response to something old is as unfamiliar to you as a foreign land. In other words, you wouldn't recognize that land of creativity, even if you visited it.

If there were a secret decoder ring for interpreting dreams, (there isn't, but if there were) it would be the feelings invoked by the dream. Just as in our waking reality what we *feel* is our highest wisdom. Unraveling the dream language is always best started at the feeling level of understanding. Let's take a dream where we are being chased, and a deeply fearful feeling possesses our nervous system. Even if these are the only details we remember, this is still a good starting point. Dreams in which we are being chased almost always indicate that there is something in our lives, in our unconscious mind, that we are running away from. There is something in our lives we are not facing. No one can be running away from something, and facing something at the same time. So what is it that we are running from? The feelings tell us if it is something we have stored in our minds as scary. Something with more power than ourselves. Something that will not just go away harmlessly. Feelings are the best way to begin to integrate dream commentary.

There are a few dream details I have noticed to be fairly universal. Wood, Fire, Water, Earth, Metal and Wind are universal Elements. As such, these elements mean the same thing in Indian Ayurvedic medicine as they do in Chinese medicine. When these Elements appear in dreams, (and they do frequently) the best place to 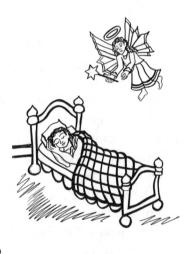 start is with a universal understanding of the element itself.

The Wood Element is associated with the liver and gall bladder in the physical body. It is not limited to these organs. These are simply the primary ones. The Wood Element is about growth and expansion: Anything that gets cut off and then grows back. When the Wood Element is out of balance it can attack the Earth Element. The energy in the liver literally expands and attacks the neighboring spleen, which is Earth Element. When the emotional side of Wood is out of balance, anger, resentment, bitterness and defensiveness are the divine visitors that are attracted. When the Wood Element is balanced the emotional visitors will be wisdom, understanding and tolerance. The enemy of Wood is the Wind Element.

The Fire Element is associated with the heart and the small intestines. Again these are merely the primary physical organs. The Fire Element is known for its double-edged sword. Fire destroys or purges, or it starts energy anew. For example when a fire rages through a redwood forest, the fire destroys existing trees. However the fire also incubates and activates redwood seedlings under the Earth. In this way, fire simultaneously destroys and initiates a new beginning. Another example would be the Phoenix Bird that dies on the funeral pyre while arising from the ashes. Out of balance Fire emotions will be impatience, irritability, pushiness and again, defensiveness. Balanced Fire emotions are patient, joyful, happy and compassionate.

The Water element relates physically to the kidneys and bladder. According to Swedenborg, water corresponds to truth in the spiritual realm. If the water in your dream is clear, easy to breath in, even while underwater, it is about a higher truth. If the water is threatening, churned up and dangerous in the dream, it is about a false truth causing difficulty for the wave. Emotionally, the Water Element is about either fear or creativity. We are either creating a new response to life by giving our attention to the truth, or we are recreating limitation by giving attention to fear-based thoughts and beliefs.

The Earth Element corresponds physically to the spleen

and pancreas. The Earth holds together and supports the Wood Element, so you can already see the potential problems if the Wood is attacking the Earth. Not good to bite the hand that supports your very existence. When the element is balanced, the emotions involved are stability, fully supported, sweetness of life and unconditionally loving. When out of balance the emotions turn into worry, anxiety, panic and feelings of being stressed out, unstable.

The Metal Element governs the lungs and large intestines in the physical body. When the Metal Element is out of balance the emotions that accumulate are grief, sadness, depression and a sense of loss. When balanced, the Metal Element is about self-confidence, courage, and self-assurance. The Metal Element is the intelligence that recognizes what is useful - what strengthens us. It releases everything else as waste.

Wind is the trickiest of the universal forces according to Shamanism, as well as Ayurveda and Chinese Medicine. Wind, when balanced, has to do with a balanced movement in life. Without Winds there would be no movement in your body. Without Wind, your heart would not beat, your eyes would not blink, your blood would not circulate. However, when out of balance, Wind internally is as destructive as an F5 hurricane is externally. Giving attention to worry, stories of *didn't do it right, not good enough or not enough*, as well as, unsupported, abandoned and unworthy generate Winds within the physical and emotional bodies. Winds are the most difficult of the universal forces to bring into balance, and can create very complex problems when provoked. Even if the other elements within the body are balanced, out-of-balanced

Wind can blow these other elements around, creating all kinds of symptoms and turmoil within the body. Eating inappropriate food combinations, such as mixing fruits with grains, fruit with dairy, or mixing animal proteins (cheese and eggs or dairy and meat), can create internal Winds and body storms. Allowing yourself to get worked up emotionally, fanning the fire of anger, or feeding worry and fear, generate internal Winds. However, giving your attention to the things that live in hell are the highest on the Wind-provoking list.

This information barely grazes the surface of this deep underlining paradigm of universal intelligence. I have given just the most basic of introductions. A more meaningful way to understand this information would be to talk with an Acupuncturist or Ayurvedic practitioner about the elements that most require balancing in your life. To glean information about the element or combination of elements that are out-of-balance in your present moment reality, is the best way to understand what these elements mean when appearing in your dream life, and your seasonal/elemental existence.

The other image I find to have a fairly consistent meaning, is a dream about cars. I've discovered cars almost always refer to one's driving force, or a commentary on how one gets around in the world. I have seen car images also mean other things. However, eight out of ten times, it is the driving force, how one gets around in the world or what drives you.

Again practice is the key in dream interpretation. Practice paying attention to how the dream made you feel. Practice letting the dream tell you why it packaged itself in a specific image or situation. This is always the best way to begin unraveling the secret world of dream wisdom.

Another fun dream technique is dream re-entry. Let's say you experienced a dream that you felt you had not finished, or a dream that you would like to explore more thoroughly. You can re-enter the dream and "play it again, Sam." The most useful technique I have found is to focus on the feeling of the dream and what visuals you remember. Keep replaying these over and over again, in your mind, as you are falling asleep. Dream re-entry is usually most effective when there has been a short passage of time between waking and dreaming states of consciousness.

If you wake up from a dream, maintain as much connection to the memory of the feelings and imagery as possible. Then, as you are drifting off, back into dreamtime, again hold the intention you want to re-enter the dream. Just understanding that these techniques are possible is oftentimes enough to start you on your dream way.

Lucid Dreaming

The techniques discussed in non-lucid dreaming apply in lucid dreaming as well. Hold the intention to remember your dreams. Hold the intention to resolve a conflict or gather additional information in dream time. However, with the practice of lucid dreaming we can now go further. We can now take the dream practice to an infinitely higher level of self-mastery.

As with non-lucid dreaming the best time to start preparing for dreamtime is during waking reality. **It is essential as you move through your everyday life, to test**

reality. Never, at anytime, is it useful to assume that you are awake. Many, many times during the day – *test* reality. There are a few ways to do this. The most common test is the reading test. I learned to carry pieces of paper in my pockets that say, "Am I dreaming?" [from the Lucidity Institute]. Then focus on something else. Then come back and try re-reading "Am I dreaming?" Then again focus on something else. Then for a third time come back to re-reading "Am I dreaming?" If you can read your test three times in a row, after focusing on something else, in between, you most likely are not dreaming.

In dream time there is no static reality. There are no dream atoms to hold dream reality together, so its very fluid nature is enough to tip you off, that you are dreaming. When I was in college, I was at a friend's house using his computer to write a school term paper. My friend's very affectionate black cat kept rubbing up against my legs as I was writing. I stopped writing and bent over to pet the cat. When I sat back upright, I noticed the computer screen had gone completely black. I could not remember when I last saved the data, so I began to panic. Had I lost the entire paper? I looked behind the computer for the reset button, I noticed it next to the small RCA metal serial number plate. I pressed the button, then checked the screen again. Nothing, still black as night. I decided to exhaust my computer expertise and press the reset button again. I looked back behind the computer saw the reset button, only this time the small metal serial number plate said Magnavox. I realized I was dreaming, and flew off to see what my lucid dream world had in store for me.

If you practice this reading test enough in waking reality, you will catch yourself in a dream and make use of it to become lucid. I also find that just reading about dreams or lucid dreaming is enough to give your dream life a boost. Another playful reality test I enjoy is the flying test. I usually practice this one in the privacy of my own home, or at the very least when no one else is watching. I frequently fly in my lucid dream excursions, so in this test I take a running jump and try to take off flying. Many times the pull of gravity, in waking reality, cuts the trip short, so I know I'm not dreaming. However a number of times I have shocked myself to discover I'm in mid-flight!

In lucid dreaming you can walk up walls and walk through solid objects. These are a bit harder to test without hurting yourself, should it turn out you're not dreaming. So if you want to practice testing reality along these lines, I suggest you do it with something of a softer nature. Do not jump off the roof to test dream-flight – Try something that is no big deal if you are not dreaming. When you make your bed in the morning try putting your hand through your pillow. I also try to put my hand through the shower curtain when showering. The idea is to incorporate something you do everyday as a reality test. The more you do some thing in your everyday life, the more likely it is to show up in dreamtime.

Establishing a lucid dream goal before you become lucid is critical. Consider what you want to know or where you want to go before becoming lucid in a dream. Often what will happen is that the first few times you become lucid in a dream, you are so excited to have managed making a connection to that state of mind, you wake yourself up. If you have planned your trip you are better able to make use of your time there. For example, I usually hold the intention that I want to go wherever Heaven would like me to go. Then I just jump up and start flying. I know that

Heaven will direct the aspect of mind I'm going to dance with in this lucid dream trip.

I learned some invaluable lucid dreaming techniques from dream master Dr. Stephen LaBerge. I most highly recommend reading *anything* written by Dr. LaBerge. His techniques are tried and true. A couple of tips Stephen passed on, were how to remain lucid after you become lucid. The first is to have a plan. When I first started working with the great folks at the Lucidity Institute at Stanford University, I was experiencing some health challenges. Dr. LaBerge suggested that after becoming lucid, I ask dream characters what the health problems were related to. He suggested I ask not only the people dream characters, but animals as well as plants. Any image that appears in the dream has information.

I remember once after rehashing a dream, Dr. LaBerge turned to me and said, "If you want to experience something really interesting in a dream, look for a staircase or elevator and take it up or down." Dr. LaBerge insisted the more unexpected journeys would happen if I went down into the unconscious mind. I have never forgotten his advice. Anytime I am presented with this opportunity in a lucid dream, I take it.

While dreaming, I inspect my dream body to see what it looks like. I have gained many insights about what the waking physical body needs by interviewing the dream body for information. Asking questions in a lucid dream is always a wild ride. **The first rule of lucid dreaming is that your dream characters will always surprise you with their answers and comments.** I like to ask anything appearing in a lucid dream: "Who are you?" "Who am I?" "What can I do for you?" "What do you want me to know?" "Is there some place that you want us to travel to?" "Can you help me to be more awakened?" "Can you teach me about the lucid dream world?" "How can you help me achieve happiness?"

There are some exercises Dr. LaBerge asks everyone in his program to try. Having sex with a dream character is one of them. I found this exercise very, very challenging. **The purpose of sex in a dream, lucid or otherwise, is self-integration.** The Polynesian people are very advanced dream workers. They highly encourage sexual activity in dreamtime. The idea is to make all aspects of your mind a successful intimate partner in your life. This may sound elementary. However, most unrealized waves have divided their minds against themselves because of the use of thoughts and beliefs. Having sex in a dream is a union-forming action, generating great internal healing.

The general rule is that anything you do in waking reality will be easier to do in dreamtime. So I figured this sex thing was a piece of cake. Wrong! The first few times I became lucid with this intention, I could not find anything, male or female, human or otherwise, I would have sex with on a bet. Then after a number of months of trying, I lowered my expectations. I started asking anything that moved if it would engage in a sexual activity. Every last dream character I asked told me, "Nope, not interested." It took me nearly a year, making my mind my friend, before I was able to consummate that dream assignment!

Perpetuating a lucid dream is another tip I learned at the Lucidity Institute. Many times you can see and feel the lucid dream begin to disintegrate, as opposed to just waking up. When you feel the dream start to break up, spin your dream body like a top, or perform cartwheels. Anything that would disturb your inner ear while awake will reintegrate the dream reality. Sometimes the reintegration only holds for a few seconds; other times this technique can extend the dream for much longer.

There is also the issue of false awakenings, and I would be remiss if I did not at least touch upon it. That is where you think and believe you have awakened, but you are in reality still very much asleep. This experience is also referred to as "nested dreaming." This happens much, much more frequently than one imagines. Having a digital clock is very helpful. I cannot tell you how many times I thought I was awake, only to glance at the clock and see the time was 45:45. Clearly there is no such time. Clearly I was only dreaming that I was awake. **Never assume you are awake! Never assume you know what reality is!** Always ask reality to tell you something about its self-evident nature. Always be ready to learn from an open and neutral mindset. Always wear a humble and impartial undergarment; it never chaffs or forms a wedgie, unless you dream it too!

I have noticed that colors are much brighter in lucid dreams. There are no words for the powerful feelings of integration and fearlessness that one feels after waking from a lucid dream. The understanding and embodiment of the wisdom that we are all creating this world from mind. That this reality is, but a dream within a dream, becomes unmistakable, tangible and clear after a lucid dream. There is enough value in that realization alone to practice this dream skill.

You can form a dream play circle where friends and like-minded people can get together, share dream experiences and possible dream interpretations. This is always a positive way to empower the dream practice as well. One of the many spiritual teachers I have studied with used to say that the purpose and meaning of life is to share more. That is why God divided Itself into many God selves. Now there is more to share and more to share with. Share more fun! Share more play! Share more love. Share more dreams! Share on, wild one!

The following is a copy of a dream journal I made years ago. I have included it as an example of how to use the dream techniques we discussed in this section. Enjoy reading *In Search of Swedenborg*. See you in dreamtime!

In Search of Swendenborg

By Vaishali

I follow my dreams. This is perhaps not the strangest thing in the world to hear someone say, but when your nocturnal visitations advise you that the time has come to move out of your home, pack up all your possessions, and move from one person's house to the next, thereby forming the "Mobile Blessing Business," the implications can get pretty weird!

Just exactly how do one's dreams go about soliciting such eccentric behavior, and why should anyone in their right mind choose to follow such advice? Well, in my case, it all started when I made a trip to the bathroom, in a dream of course. Taking advice based on dream information and executing a life strategy in accordance with dream time wisdom is older than Joseph and Pharaoh. If you recall, Pharaoh ordered a food storage program strictly based on Joseph's interpretation of one of his dreams. I was at the University I was attending, waiting in an endlessly long line to get to the ladies room, when I looked around and noticed that all the bathrooms on Campus had incredibly long lines. I made some comment along the lines of, "Hey, what gives? Do all great bladders think alike?" The women in line around me responded with very strange looks, as if I should know something, but didn't and they were embarrassed for me.

One woman finally pulled me aside and explained to me that this is the time of the month, at noon, when the entire student body stands in line at the bathrooms, and each student awaits their turn. Then, one-by-one, the students file in until all the stalls are filled, then the bathrooms are closed and permeated with gas. The students inside are asphyxiated, their dead bodies removed, and this morbid procedure is then repeated for the period of an hour, at which time all the remaining students return to their classes.

I'm shocked. With my dream mouth gapping open and in a stammering voice I attempt to talk these people out of flushing their lives away. "You don't have to do this!" I cry. "You can choose not to be suicidal bathroom lemmings!" I implore. But the students standing around me are unmoved by my existential pontifications. Frustrated beyond words as to why anyone would be so compliant with such an insane ritual, I finally leave and go in search of more rational life-forms.

Then I go to a restaurant and approach a waitress who is wiping down a table. I ask her if the community at large knows what is going on: students are killing themselves in bathrooms! She finished cleaning the table, casually flips the towel over her shoulder, looks me right in the eye, and says, "Yes, the community knows. But they're all Oriental, so who cares?" The shock of her words send me rushing headlong into waking reality, and I find myself sitting upright in bed, rigidly aghast at the scenario my mind has just played out for me, in living, vivid, racist color.

I worked on that dream for days, trying to unravel what the hell my dreaming mind had against all the Asian students at school. I have come up with a few insights that I felt in my heart and gut were shallow and missing the point completely. A couple of nights later, I awoke to find myself sitting up in bed and saying aloud to no one in particular, "It's not 'Oriental' . . . it's 'all mental'!'"

Suddenly, the whole thing fell into place! I had come to a realization earlier that I had been living far too much of my life in my head. In other words, there are other kinds of "knowing" besides the simple solutions that the brain secretes. Intuition, for example. How many times have you had a gut feeling to do one thing, but your brain disagreed and came back with, "No, don't listen to that gut feeling. That's for jerks and new-age losers. Do what I tell you." Do you go against your gut's knowing only to have the whole thing blow up in your face, leaving your dick in the dirt, and your intuition screaming, "I told you so, you mental dweeb!" If real life experience had taught me anything, it is that the brain can rationalize away anything.

The human brain is like a good secretary: it can take notes, type things, file notes, and make photocopies. Yes, that's something a secretary does very well, lots and lots of photocopying. But when it comes right down to owning and running the business, it just simply isn't enough. The entire human experience is needed to keep the business in the black. The secretary is good as long as it is used as a reliable helper and not as the pilot, navigator, or driving force.

Since that startling moment of mental self-revelation, I have been trying to move my life out of my head and expand it to include other forms of "knowing" the human experience has to offer. Through the imagery of the student body, my dream was confirming that I was indeed removing the mental body from the driver's seat, which had so far done a great job of driving me right into the shitter. I was now starting to think on a more integrated level, and not just exclusively with my brain. The imagery of the waitress suddenly became patently clear as well: when I went to a part of myself that serves me, the waitress, and asked, "Does the community at large know that a part of the community is choking on its own hot air." The answer was, "Yes, but it's all the mental part, so who cares?" In other words, it's okay. This is what you wanted to do, so don't let the brain panic you, as it is accustomed to running this show, and it will not go down without reciting its rational, rattled rhetoric over its removal. The ego can be such a sore loser.

Shortly afterwards, I began to have a series of dreams that visually foretold how to construct the "Mobile Blessing Business." These dreams offered rather simple ideas on how to run such a business, where I move from one home to another, not spending more than one, on rare occasions two, evenings in any one person's home. And when I followed these instructions, to the utter bewilderment and astonishment of my rational mind, I found my calendar booked up two and three weeks in advance.

When I listened to my dreams, I found I could do no wrong. People would call me up after spending one evening with them, and ask how soon I could come back and spend another night. Or I would get a call from someone saying that their life had not been going well lately, and they knew if they could just have another visit from the Mobile Blessing Biz things would get better.

Every time I would get another call or request, my brain would look at my month booked up in advance and say, "Who would have thought it?" and indeed, who would have thought such a thing? Well, apparently our dreams seem to know more about our lives then our waking clueless mind does, which is what scientist/mystic Emanuel Swendenborg realized in his work with dreams. After learning about Swedenborg's life and dream work, he quickly became one of my favorite philosophers.

Swedenborg, who died in 1772, was a member of Sweden's Parliament, a metallurgist and scientist, who mastered every known science in his life. Swedenborg is the one who came up with the idea of the lunar form of longitude and latitude. He figured out what the cerebellum in the human brain is for. He wrote three volumes on the human brain, and 150 other scientific works on everything from fire and color, to soil erosion. It wasn't, however, until Swedenborg was well into his fifties that his "other" talents became public.

Swedenborg had been able to control his breathing since he was a small child, and entered into trance-like states. Then, suddenly, at the age of 56, he broke through into the spiritual realm, and traveled into what he said were various levels of Heaven and hell. Swedenborg did this every day until he died, and wrote volumes and volumes of work recording his discourse with higher and lower order spirits. According to Swedenborg, dreams are where Spirits, or Angels, come and speak to you in a symbolic language that is constantly commenting on the quality of your life. In other words, dreams are more than just picking through the shit of your daily routine; dreams are a way of picking up a direct line to the Divine to see what IT has to say to you about your life.

And in my dreams, as in Abraham's life, the Divine was asking me to sacrifice something, in my case, it was a mailing address, and to make that leap of faith to a place where the rational brain can't take you. And, like Abraham, once I made the faithful swan dive, the Divine came through with Issac, or in my case, the Mobile Blessing Business.

It was about this time that Dr. Stephen LaBerge, Stanford University's lucid dream scientist whiz kid, who wrote *Lucid Dreaming,* had come out with a new book, co-written by Howard Rheingold, *Exploring the World of Lucid Dreaming.* LaBerge laid out very simple, easy-to-follow, step-by-step ideas on how to become lucid in one's dreams. Lucid dreaming is where the dreamer knows that they are asleep and that what they are experiencing is a dream. This state of lucidity allows the dreamer to interact with their dreams and dream characters on a much more conscious level of self-integration, as the dreamer has complete access to all their waking memories. In other words, in a lucid dream, because I know that I'm dreaming, I can use the mock dream world to create the perfect world simulator, and try out or explore any scenario possible, with no facility fees or risk of physical or emotional injury – my own dream holo-deck!

LaBerge, who had gone on to start The Lucidity Institute, has since come up with a very clever invention called the DreamLight. Now, the DreamLight is where dreamland and high technology make for very interesting bedfellows. The DreamLight is a mask-like device that the "would-be dreamer" wears very comfortably to bed. Once the dreamer has hit REM (rapid eye movement), the stage of sleep where one dreams, the mask will flash a light acting as a visual cue bringing the sleeper to the realization that they are indeed asleep and dreaming, thus enabling them to become lucid.

For the serious dreamworker, this makes the DreamLight quite possibly the most exciting thing they could take to bed with them. With the help of the DreamLight, I could learn how to become lucid at will! And bearing this idea in mind, a casual sit-down diner conversation with Swedenborg could only be a dream away, through dreamtime travel.

On another level of stimulation, if I want to have sex with the partner or multiple partners of my choice, the DreamLight can provide it. If I want to rap with Einstein on how to solve a problem, or share my innermost longings with Freud, the DreamLight can arrange it. If I want to conquer the world with Alexander the Great, fly to the moon, or visit another planet, the DreamLight can stamp my passport in the blink of a dream eye.

Sure, an intense drug trip or virtual reality experience might offer a person an unrestrained, exuberant, excessive sensual experience, but in comparison this stimulus will always fall short of the benefits to be had from a lucid dream. And the reason for this is simple: all characters and images that one encounters during a lucid dream are fragments of the dreamer's personality. Therefore, if I have an erotic encounter with the dream partner of my choice, not only am I enjoying the safest and best sex I will ever know in my life (because lets face it, folks, no one knows how to give it to you like you do!), I am also gratifying myself on the deepest level of self-integration possible. In other words, when you make love to a dream character, you are making love to a part of yourself that is screaming out for love, attention, and nurturing.

I contacted LaBerge and arranged to use the Dream-Light for a period of time, in return for which I would complete the necessary paperwork and assist the Lucid-ity Institute in gathering research from lucid dreamers to perfect the DreamLight before putting it out in the market. Over the months of working with them, I found that LaBerge and Lynn Levitan, the DreamLight's chief shaman, as well as the other associates of The Lucidity Institute, are all incredible well-balanced, self-integrated, and down right likeable people. They are truly walking testimonials to the benefits of lucid dreaming. Always a good sign, when the promoters of self-exploration and discovery are worth the endorsement they're printed on.

After going over the basic DreamLight flying instructions with Lynn, I clutched the dream detecting device to my breast, like it was my first born child and dashed off to sleep, perchance to lucidly dream. I didn't have to wait long. After a few nights, I had my first blown Dream-Light induced lucid dream. It was a self-confrontational doozy.

The dream started out non-lucidly, recalling what hap-pen just before becoming lucid, I remember, I dreamt, I was walking through a parking lot late at night. When all of a sudden Don Henley opened a car door and got out. He asked me if I wanted to jump in the back seat and have sex with him. As I was contemplating the offer, I leaned over and looked into the backseat where I saw that Don had already corralled two very young girls (I'd have to say they were fighting for every bit of thirteen, may been fourteen, years old). I looked back, shaking my head at Don, who smiled anxiously and rubbed his hands together. "Sorry, babe," I told him, "but you're just too sleazy, even for me." Moments after leaving Don and his tuck and roll den of iniquity, the DreamLight flashed. I stopped dead in my tracks, extended my arms towards Heaven and shouted excitedly, "I'm dreaming!" I then leapt into the air and began to fly.

I have found from experience that the manipulation of things – objects or images in lucid dreams – is not the way to go. First of all, there is a huge limit to what one can manipulate, and secondly, just as in waking reality, the best course of action is always to change yourself and your attitude and leave the rest of the world to its own devices. In other words, the name of the game is to master yourself and not the world; or, depending on how you look at it, by mastering yourself, you have mastered the world. With this basic dream philosophy in mind, what I find the most beneficial is to speak aloud a request, and then go off in a random direction and see what finds me.

Immediately, after taking into the air, I found myself flying over a forest at night. Below me was a cabin with a light on. I had been repeating the thought that I wanted to meet with Swedenborg while flying, so I was very curious to drop in and investigate. Inside the cabin which was packed from floor to ceiling with stacks of papers and files, was one human looking man seated on the floor, and another non-human looking, reddish-brown creature with pointed ears who was busy shuffling papers, moving files, and such from one side of the cabin to the other.

The human-looking creature looked up and in a very flat nasal monotone voice asked, "Are you Vaishali?" I nodded yes, and he handed me a postcard. "This is for you." I tried to read it but the handwriting was very difficult to read, and the words followed no order that made any sense (I don't recall if the postcard was signed or not). I looked back at the two of them; they were still hard at work shuffling papers, and I asked them, "Who are you?" The human-looking one informed me that his name was "Wormwood". I experienced a flash of realization as the reddish-brown creature and I, in unison, responded with "Screwtape" in perfect chorus. Knowing who, or rather *what*, they were (characters from a C.S. Lewis book I was not to read until years later, *The Screwtape Letters*), I decided then that I didn't want to hang out with them anymore. "Well," I said as I was leaving, "tell C.S. Lewis I said 'Hello'." Without looking up from his mountain of paperwork, Wormwood acknowledged he would pass along my greeting.

I then started to fly again and continue to seek Swedenborg. I spied another house and descended. Upon entering the house, I found it to be a very large, cozy wooden home with lots of booked-lined shelves, large, thick oriental rugs, and a black grand piano. It appeared to be empty except for a big black dog with an unusually long snout and rows of sharp white teeth. As I approached the dog, I remembered a conversation with LaBerge about how dream characters and images responded to the dream's expectations. So I extended my hand, speaking very softly in a friendly tone, expecting the dog to respond similarly. Instead, the dog began to snarl. The thought of 'Oh, fuck this shit!" crossed my mind just before I kicked the dog down a flight of stairs and out of my way.

At this point, the dream began to decay, so I started to spin my dream body, which is a technique to reintegrate the lucidity of a dream. The first attempt didn't do much, so I tried it again and ended up falling backward. As I was lying on the floor looking upward, I noticed a small group of men and women entering the room. As I was getting up, I remembered thinking, "Okay, now we're getting somewhere!"

I stood up and checked out the people. It seemed fairly equally divided among men and women (about three or four each). I went over and tried to talk with them, but they all seemed very disinterested in my conversation. The men and women split up. I followed the women. There was a woman in her fifties or sixties, a blonde woman in a starched white blouse with a high neck and long sleeves, and another dark-haired woman who I don't recall very well. I started a conversation with the older woman about my health, as I had been experiencing liver and intestinal problems. I asked her, "if you were me, what would you do?" the woman quite obviously didn't want to talk about it. Finally, she blurted out, "If you're asking me, it's utterly impossible!" I was somewhat shocked, this is not what I was expecting. I was expecting a straight forward answer from a concerned interactive dream character. This is not what I got.

I looked over at the blonde woman and noticed she had

her arms crossed defiantly in front of her, and was glaring at me. You're Cindy Lou, aren't you?" she questioned rather sternly (Cindy Lou is the name my parents gave me at birth). I nodded yes. "Well," she said, "I'm the Lou," meaning she was the "Lou" of "Cindy Lou." I have always thought of the "Lou" part, of the "Cindy Lou" name, as being the playful, childlike part of my personality, but this uptight woman with an attitude problem, in her starched white, high-collared blouse didn't strike me as very playful or fun. "You think you're really cute, don't you," she asked me harshly. "Yes, I do," I told her half laughing, half smiling. "I have a lot of cuteness." "Oh, dry it up, if you have it," she said sarcastically behind her still folded arms. "Dry it up, if you have it," I said while pounding my fist onto the counter in amusement. "That's very funny. I'll have to remember to steal that." "Steal that," Lou snorted, "you said it!" I then began to ask Lou about my health, and what would she do in my place? Lou became extremely uncooperative and refused to comment. The women then completely ignored me, and started talking among themselves. Dream disaster!

I woke up at this point, very confused and very doubtful after meeting Lou, as to whether or not I really wanted to get to know myself. I didn't appear to be as charming and clever as my waking ego would like me to believe. I knew I was going to be driving over to Stanford the next day, so I though I'd ask LaBerge if he would mind setting aside some time to run this one by his discerning dream mind. I wanted to tell him about the unexpected resistance I encountered with my dream characters, when I followed his advice on how to approach questioning them.

Being unexpectedly very generous with his time, La-Berge suggested that Lynne, Daryl Hewitt, a highly accomplished lucid dreamer and sleep subject of LaBerge's, and I go out to dinner and discuss this matter at length in a more relaxed environment. Over a steaming piece of vegetarian pizza, I retold my encounter with Wormwood and Screwtape. When I got to the part about kicking the dog down the stairs, LaBerge interrupted me, saying, "You kicked whatever is eating your liver down the stairs." "Huh?" I replied, looking as vacant as all of interstellar space. "That dog you kicked down the stairs is YOU. Why didn't you talk with it, ask the dog why it is snarling? After all, what kind of noises does your gut make when it's upset?" at this, very dim light bulb appeared over my previously dark mind and began to glow brighter. "Well," I answered slowly, "it certainly doesn't purr."

Suddenly, I realized that I had been carrying the model of the waking world with me into my dreams, and allowing myself to be limited by those restrictions. In my dreams, dogs can talk, and I can understand them! I my dreams, I have nothing to fear as the wild, untamed animals of my mind can rip into my dream flesh and not hurt me a bit. This is the time to tame those watchdogs of my inner sanctums, to make them my friends and allies, not to blow the dream opportunity by kicking them down the dream stairs.

"You've been looking for answers about yourself!" LaBerge continued, "but when you come across them, if they don't respond as you would like them to you kick them down stairs. Could it be that you are doing this in your waking life?" A painful and all true question that had not occurred to me when I put the dream through my own waking consciousness filter. Here I am, looking to 'know thyself;' yet when I come across glimpses of myself, I push myself downstairs and out of the way, in the name of trying to find myself! The human condition . . . it's just loaded with laughs! Suddenly, I caught a brief insight as to how the Buddha must have felt sitting under that now famous Bodhi tree, calmly facing the most heinous reflections that his own mind could possibly hurtle at him. Like an angry Mara, complete with an army of demon's, thirst for blood, wanting only to tear him savagely apart, limb-from-limb. Could I become as non-attached to these dream images as the Buddha did to his mental projections and illusions, in order to become "awakened" on some level? Well, in the dream world, I have the perfect simulator in which to practice. Not only do I get the opportunity to face these masterfully hidden facets of self by the waking ego, but I get to do it in an environment in which I am immortal, impervious to pain or bodily damage!

While still picking at my first piece of pizza (self-revelation and honesty aren't always the easiest things to swallow and digest), I continued with my dream story. By talking about it and handling it with other dreamers, I could see various dream elements with a perspective unlimited by my own ego's ever-looming, ever-shifting blind-spots. Then, in mid-thought stream it suddenly struck me. "Wait a minute," I said, "the dog didn't come back up the stair after I kicked it down." "The dog didn't come back as the dog," LaBerge pointed out, "but maybe it came back as those men and women that came into the room." "Oh, holy shit!" I exclaimed while attempting to knock some sense into my forehead with my open palm. "That would explain why they were not terribly interested in talking with me . . . I just got done kicking them down the stairs." At that moment I knew what conclusions my dream images must have come to about me. "Here comes the God Almighty conscious mind, in its infinite wisdom, kicking the shit out of everything it comes across – what a fucking asshole!" Yep, the old saying, "We have seen the enemy, and it is us" has never been truer.

This would also explain Lou's reaction to me: utter disgust for this disruptive ego/personality that barges in and starts pushing everything it doesn't like downstairs; to add insult to injury, it has the audacity to think it's being fashionably cute while doing it! No wonder I wasn't overjoyed to see myself, or talk playfully with myself; no wonder the older woman version of me did little more than verbally shoot me the "bird!"

Like the coyote at another failed attempt at catching the roadrunner, I sat back down at the old dream drawing board, and tried to come up with another plan to search for Swedenborg, and maybe discover a bit more of myself along the way.

A few nights later, I got my chance with my second DreamLight lucid dream. I dreamt that I had purchased a few things for an interview I was doing, and I found that I didn't need any of the things that I had bought, so I went back to the store to return them. As I was waiting in line, the DreamLight mask flashed and this started to wake me up enough to realize that I was dreaming.

When the saleswoman turned to look at me, her gaze was very penetrating and intense (like I was seeing myself). She asked me why I was returning the items, which struck me at the time as a very deep and profound question. I thought about it a moment, and then responded cheerfully, "I'm returning these things because I've discovered that I don't need them!" In other words, I discovered that I did not need to invest in devices outside of myself to be in the world . . . I'm enough all by myself! The saleswoman seemed just as pleased and understanding of this revelation as I was.

I then left the store and began walking down a long white corridor, thinking about how real this mock dream world appeared. The corridor was under a large building, and when I stopped to put my hand near the wall I would feel the coldness that was seeping out from the concrete. As I continued walking, the sound of my footfalls was incredibly, hauntingly real. I could even see my hands swinging by my side, out of the corner of my eye. A man appeared from around the corner and was walking toward me. His appearance, although not terrifying, did frighten me. He looked somewhat alien. He had a largish bald head and golden-yellow eyes; his face was expressionless. As we got closer and closer, I remembered that I had a dream body and could not be hurt by this man. I also recalled my latest conversation with LaBerge about how "loving your enemies" works in dreams. So I began thinking, "This is a part of myself that I am just less familiar with, love and accept this particular new self." I repeated this thought over and over again until the feeling welled up organically within me.

As we got within arms reach of each other, I put all my awareness into the thought, "love yourself, love yourself, love yourself." At that moment, I felt I was truly loving and accepting this somewhat alien image of myself. The man then turned to look at me and smiled warmly; I smiled back as we passed each other.

I continued down the hall where I encountered a younger man. As soon as we saw each other, we immediately exchanged kind, warm smiles and glances. I passed this man to make my way to a large set of double doors just behind him. I exited the corridor, and found myself walking up a flight of stairs leading to a big, beautiful lobby of a huge skyscraper-like building. I was excitedly dashing up the stairs, taking them two at a time, when I felt the muscles in the back of my leg straining. This brought to my attention the absurdity of walking and I immediately began to fly. As I pushed myself up off the floor, I heard a slight woosh sound (like the kind the Enterprise makes at the beginning of the original Star Trek).

As I was flying, I decided I wanted to go see Swedenborg. So I continued rising upward. There was a big, beautiful, domed, stained-glass window covering the lobby, and I flew right through it, moving ever upward. However, I did not find myself outside. Instead, I found myself in another store. So I flew though the ceiling of that store into another. This went on for about three or four stores. Finally, I sat down on the floor, my legs dangling down through the hole I had just made, and thought, "You know there has got to be a better way to get to Swedenborg." I looked back down through the series of holes I had made bursting up through the ceilings and floors and saw a few people walking around below. I had just made up my mind to fly back down and check out the people milling below, when the entire dreamscape went black and I woke up.

Well, I hadn't met Swedenborg yet, but I did seem to have jumped and cleared a "love thyself" hurdle I had been tripping over for years. The next lucid dream the DreamLight delivered to my mental doorstep was unlike anything I've ever dreamt of before or since.

I was in the midst of a dream when the DreamLight mask flashed. The flashing light left me with the realization that I was in fact asleep and dreaming, but something else happened, or rather didn't happen. In this dream, not only was I not any specific character when I became lucid, but I never, at any time, developed my own individual dream body or ego. In other words, there was no "Vaishali," per se.

The dream was about a group of dancers acting out an elaborate concert piece. One character expressed Life, while another did the dance of Death; one would be Love, another Hatred. The movement of yet another dancer would become Redemption, while a different dancer's motion spoke of Revenge. These representations would flow, merge, weave, and ebb amongst each other, until each dancer exchanged and finally became all roles, each taking their turn to create a larger whole. In this way, it was as if the entire life/death dance of Shiva was lived, expressed, felt, and ultimately shared by all the dancers.

All during the body poetry in motion, "I" was all the dancers at once, all the time. There was no individual "self;" more than that, there was not even the slight trace of any recollection that there should be any separation of "self." At no time did I think, "Gee, this is weird, you know I really should have my own body, my own ego, my own separate identity." Instead, the images of these beautifully long, slender bodies all streaming upward and flowing gracefully around each other seemed more normal and natural than the individual ego separated by waking reality.

Yes, I was asleep, and yes, I was actually lucidly dreaming, but something else was going on here, some level of self-integration the likes of which I have never known before. If was as if for the first time, I truly understood Zen Buddhism. The perfect experience of pure being, knowing no separation of self, experiencing all things as One. Equally in line with, the concept of Zen, words cannot be used to describe it; furthermore, the application of words to the experience is actually misleading. As it was not like this or that . . . it just simply was: an experience of prefect being, completely seamless with no separation or boundaries, beyond fear and desire.

Since the Zen dream, I had gone back to searching for Swedenborg, employing different ideas and techniques that have worked for other lucid dreamers. In my search, I shared a park bench with Toulouse-Lautrec, who I found to be very charming, witty, and quite the ladies man. I met with Geroge Burns in the "control room" of my mind, who wrapped his kindly arm around my shoulder and offered to explain the meaning of life. And countless other less famous, but certainly no less revealing, or amusing fragments of myself.

As for my latest lucid search for Swedenborg, here is how that story goes. I found myself floating and rotating effortlessly in an inky black void. I began to call out Swedenborg's name and found myself suddenly in a house. As no one seemed to be at home, I climbed the closest staircase in search of a phone. The stairs led to a small parlor in what appeared to be a Victorian house. Sunshine streamed through white lace curtains, flooding the room with light. Under the window was a table cluttered with little silver boxes, gadgets, knick-knacks, doodads, and devices, things I'd never seen before. Being continuously fascinated by bright, shiny objects, I became momentarily mesmerized by the brilliant sparkling sunlight as it danced over the finely polished silver surfaces.

Suddenly, I realized that I had been on the prowl for

a phone. I glanced around the room, spotted a phone in the corner, and went over to it. I felt an uncomfortable mixture of both excitement and apprehension as I picked up the receiver; after all, I know this is a dream and dream phones do not have to function under the same laws as phones do in waking reality. This phone might work, and it might not. It might respond with a dial tone, or it might only play Barry Manilow hits. Then again, it could be a hotline to the Oval Office or the Bat Cave. I was incredibly relieved and pleased to hear a dial tone when I put the receiver to my ear. Then, thinking I had nothing else to lose, I dialed the operator. The phone rang and a pleasant voice answered. "Operator, how can I help you?" "I want to talk to Swedenborg" I blurted out to the female voice on the other end. "One moment, please." My palmed started to sweat, and a slight tingling sensation ran up my spine when the line began to ring. Finally! I thought. At last, I have done it! I'm going to talk with Swedenborg!

My chest began to tighten, when after the second or third ring, the line was finally answered. "Hi, this is Emanuel Swedenborg, I'm not in right now, but," his answering machine! I can't believe it. I'd been shot down in flames by an answering machine!

Oh well, I thought, at least I can leave a message. Just at that very moment, every last silver box, gadget, knick-knack, doodad, and device exploded in an orchestrated burst of clicks, clangs, buzzes, and whirling noises. The room was instantly filled with the high frequency screech of many small metal objects striking, scraping, and clattering against many other small metal objects.

"That tears it!" I shouted aloud as I threw the receiver

back down on its cradle in utter disgust. I began to search the house for someone, anyone, who could explain this obnoxious post modern experience.

I stomped determinedly back down the stairs and found a man with short, very bright orange-red hair and large, luminous blue eyes waiting for me at the bottom. "Do you know who Swedenborg is?" I asked, immediately doing away with any small talk or polite introductions. He nodded yes, and with a sweeping gesture of his arm pointed off to the left and said, "He lives in a small house on the edge of my property, not far from here." "Well, I want to see him!" I half implored, half sternly stated. The nameless man looked down for a moment and shook his head no. Then he lifted his eyes to meet mine and said, "Swedenborg is very busy . . . " The dream decays here and I awakened.

During the short period of time I have used the Dream-Light, it has advanced my dream work ahead by decades, helping me to train myself to have lucid dreams on my own, without becoming a DreamLight addict. The DreamLight can help those who have never had a lucid dream to experience themselves, and to learn how to journey inwards on their own. It functions as nocturnal training wheels for the unconscious mind, without making the dreamer dependent upon the device for future growth experiences.

Since returning the DreamLight to the Lucidity Institute, I have encountered Swedenborg in my own independent lucid dream travels. Meeting him, however, only marked the beginning of my search. For I see the search for Swedenborg as symbolic of the struggle we all must engage in, to know ourselves. My search for Swedenborg is my archetypical hero's journey. And in this type of search, there never is a destination. The process is everything. We never do come to a spot where we can put up our feet and say, "I've arrived." And if you find yourself thinking that, guess what? That's right – you're going to find yourself standing right back at square one.

At any rate, I'm sure you've already figured out by now that I'm not going to stop searching for and talking with Swedenborg. Neither am I going to stop running into myself along the way, packaged in various lucid forms that only my wildest dreams could conceive of. It can be a hard path, this journey of self-discovery, full of pitfalls and tricky passes. But I'm not worried. I've got a great road map – I just keep following my dreams.

there is always infinite abundance

there is only the One,

PLAYBOOK

The Twelve Month Course

In Playfulness

M ost everyone has heard of a "Course In Miracles." Well this is a course in playfulness. The intention of this exercise is to redirect your point of view. Modern psychologists say it takes twenty-one days to establish a habit. Introduce something new into your life and repeat it for twenty-one days. This time repetition will imprint it on the human nervous system. Bearing this in mind, we are going to practice each one of the perspective changing exercises for a month. In this way we will establish a very solid happiness habit.

Please feel free to draw outside the lines. If these suggestions inspire you to modify the intention or to invent one of your own, the sky is the limit. Fly and be free! The order of these steps maybe rearranged as well, to accommodate what feels right to you.

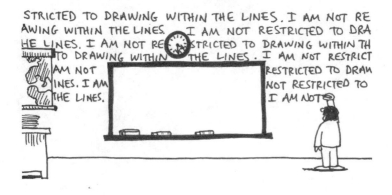

Each month, practice being/seeing the world differently. Each practice is designed to integrate the higher teachings from the book *You Are What You Love* in a practical, as well as playful, method. You do not need to act as an inner Nazi, torturing yourself if you forget and fall back into your old limited way of processing reality, unless it makes you laugh, for some, torture is a habit of fun (like working out at the gym)! Make some notes to yourself that you post on your refrigerator, bathroom mirror, or on your nightstand. Place one next to your computer screen, next to all the other reminders you have to take life far too seriously. Write love letters in the sand. The goal is to lighten up life and mind, not to give yourself one more thing to criticize yourself about. Have fun, enjoy what you are looking at . . . after all it is your own mind. After each month's exploration for creative treasure imagining, there is a blank page. This is for any moment markers you wish to make about your journey during that month's practice. There may be learning epiphanies in the moment that you wish to remind yourself of years in the future. Enjoy! Have fun! Share the treasure that is your life!

Day one we awaken to the sun, dancing has begun for healing fun in our heart and all other parts.' – Argisle

Month #1

Day one: we awaken to the sun

Imagine that everything that comes to you is perfect; it is actually coming from Heaven. Every morsel of food, every piece of mail, every request from coworkers and family members is actual food from Heaven.

It is perfect: lacking in nothing.

This does not mean that if your teenage offspring wants to go off to an orgy with unprotected sex and drug use as the scheduled entertainment, you say, "Why, yes, of course that would be perfect, go right ahead." What it does mean is that you cease looking at events and relationships as existing merely to increase the level of difficulty in your life. See this event as an opportunity to witness the interior playing itself out in the exterior. Ayurvedic psychology states that all unenlightened minds are arrested in various infantile and adolescent stages of development. The way most waves resolve this stagnancy issue is to have children and raise them. In raising the children, the wave is raising itself. See this event as the perfect opportunity to find an arrested stage and heal it. Ask yourself if there is an adolescent aspect of your own unconscious mind. That instead of requiring more of itself, simply wants to run wild without consideration of the consequences.

So if your boss comes to you and says, "We are all working late again not only tonight but all weekend." You do not necessarily keep silent about what you feel is fair and equitable. Instead, you stop and process the possibility that this event is occurring for your benefit. Stop and consider Divine Correspondence. Practice seeing the outer boss as a reflection of an inner boss that is pushing you around. Ask yourself on an inner level "Who am I really working for?" What has affected you lately that is stressful and makes you feel powerless? "How is that working for you?" Consider that, in fact, there are many opportu- nities for us to practice a higher response to life and they are being offered to us all the time. Without the practice how would we develop mastery?

Notes – Month #1

Month #2

Create a new response to all your old stories of worry and limitation. Every time you feel or become aware of worry and/or limitation working its way into your awareness, whoa! Remind yourself of **Ultimate Truth.** There is only the One. There is always infinite abundance. Remind yourself that you do not have value, power and worth. You *are* value, power and worth. These qualities are inherent, not earned. Remind yourself that you *are* love and God consciousness. Therefore you cannot create a learning experience that you do not need. Also you cannot create the learning experience before or after you need it. When is always now!

When you sense the old pattern rearing its most familiar, ugly head, remind yourself to surrender the issue to Heaven. Let Heaven know this old pattern is not what you wish to be giving your attention to. Offer it up to Heaven while you focus on showing up as a force of love in all aspects of your life. Write purifications on paper and bury it, burn it or write it on a rock and throw it in the sea then run for fun lest it come back at thee!

Constantly remind yourself to let go and let God consciousness guide you. After all you do not have the power to do anything other than create exactly what you need when you need it, in order to reach enlightenment.

Notes – Month #2

Month #3

Imagine seeing all relationships as playful. Remember Steve Irwin, the Crocodile Hunter. To him all creatures are gorgeous! This is the perfect example of keeping the realities of our life relationship lighthearted and playful. Seeing *all* relationships as playful is a spiritual necessity for a successful life. Maintaining a mindset of relationship levity keeps us in the present moment, assisting in not taking events in the temporal world personally, as well as helping us not to surrender seniority to others which renders us *less than* or inferior.

The best example of this practice is when I was called into a lawyer's office to give a deposition a few years ago. The legal people tried to maintain an air of intimidation and superiority as their first attack on a physiological level. My job was to see all relationships as playful and maintain a living connection with my own divinity and truth. I practiced, in my mind, within the privacy of my own internal dialog to see this relationship as playful. I internally adopted a Steve Irwin posture. I kept telling myself, *"I'm in the presence of a rare lawyer, a 'car accident hunting black mamba,' the most dangerous snake in the world. Isn't he gorgeous! Just look at those scales and shiny black snake eyes. This one is a real beauty, by crocky."* I held an inner air of creativity playfulness no big office filled with fancy books and overstuffed files could touch. I enjoyed silently, within my own imagination, playing with the relationship the entire time I was there to give the deposition. If anything, the opposing lawyer was frustrated with my neutrality to his usually effective intimidation techniques. Oh well, I was too busy internalizing all relationships as playful to engage in petty games of that nature.

The spiritual truth of the matter is, that *all* relationships are here to help us reach enlightenment. Since, as God consciousness, we cannot create a learning experience we do not need, we need all relationships. Seeing *all* relationships as playful is the fastest, most efficient way to accomplish this goal. Enjoy playfulness all month long! Tickle yourself silly! If assuming a Steve Irwin-like posture does not work for you, choose something else that does. Try the all-purpose Bugs Bunny persona. Always works for me. Play around with the idea. Try as many different imaginings as you need. After all you do have an entire month to try the playful persona on for size.

Notes – Month #3

Month #4

Speak in good faith to everyone you meet, *including your-self.* Ultimate Truth is that there is only the One; there is always infinite abundance. Spiritual reality is that you do not have love and God consciousness; **you are love and God consciousness.** This means that you are not capable of creating anything that does not ultimately aid you and others in reaching enlightenment. This requires that we speak the truth and we do this by speaking good faith under all circumstances and conditions. We no longer advocate for "whatever can go wrong will." We let go of our consistent inner negative ranting.

What's your favorite "let go?"

Replace the negativity with the truth, "I do not have love, I am love. Everything I am looking at is God conscious-ness in motion reaching enlightenment the fastest most efficient way it can, because it does not have the power to do anything else. Everything in the temporal world is working for me. That is why it was created - to aid mind in the process of liberation. Everything touching the nervous system is the perfect food of divine love and wisdom. That is the only power I recognize, and I am eternally grateful."

There is nothing more powerful than what we are giving our attention to. Make it positive. Make it playful. Make it based on Ultimate Truth. Make it come from the Heart, not the head. Make it a gift of good faith. Make it your next month-long practice.

Notes – Month #4

Month #5

Practice speaking and sharing gratitude for every lesson and every moment, unconditionally. Everything happens by permission of the most powerful force in the universe: divine love and wisdom. That is what makes it the most powerful force. It wins! It determines the movement of all things. Nothing has seniority over it. Therefore recognizing the truth in all things will set your mind free. Practicing an attitude of gratitude is the fastest way to align your attention with the realization that everything comes to us for our benefit, or it would not be allowed to happen. Everything that occurs is an opportunity to practice giving our attention to what lives in Heaven until that is all we know, feel and live. The planet Earth is the arena we have been given to experience this.

In the story of *Pollyanna*, the main character plays a game. It is called the "glad game." It might as well be called the "gratitude game" because in essence, that is what it is. The game is played like this: Whenever something happens, be it good or bad, we say why we are glad for it. I will start.

"I am glad that Heaven saw fit for me to lose the car accident trial because it has given me the opportunity to practice realizing that I am beyond the grasp and annihilation of the temporal world. I am grateful that things turned out the way they did. Because of the way events unfolded, I have met my life partner. I have, through him, encountered additional healers who have made all the difference in the quality of my life. I would rather be healed, whole and have a high quality of life, than to have won the trial. I could have missed out on the big win, which is my relationships with the people around me who love me and assist me in living a higher existence!" Truly the best revenge is a happy and healthy life.

Now, it is your turn. Do not empower and re-enforce complaining. Free your mind instead! Practice this next month - speaking and living only an attitude of gratitude. Practice seeing only the good and positive things coming your way; see only the gift. Give your attention only to the highest. Feel only the support of divine love and wisdom.

Notes – Month #5

Month #6

Remind yourself and others that as God consciousness, the temporal world has no power over you. This does not mean I am going to jump off the roof of a high-rise, because gravity has nothing on me. It means practice realizing that as **God consciousness everything was constructed for the convenience of your liberation**. Instead of giving your attention to what you do not want, focus on what you do want. Practice seeing yourself as beyond what happens here on the rock. Remind yourself that you are nothing temporal, nothing limited, nothing physical. You are eternal love that is beyond change. The body, experiences, belief systems and opinions, emotions - all these things are temporal and subject to change, frequent change. You are eternal. You are divine love. You can let what is limited and temporal come and go, without taking it personally and without identifying with it.

An example of this practice would be choices you have in handling pain due to illness or injury. Consider the challenges of actor Christopher Reeves. After the devastating horse accident that injured his spinal cord, Reeves wanted to die. His beautifully devoted wife asked him to please choose life. If he was not happy with that choice after some practice, she would help him in any way she could. With practice Reeves learned to say "yes" to life and life independent of the tyranny of the temporal world. He had stated that the gift of physical immobility in relationship to his children is that he now listens to them, instead of merely doing things with them.

Remind yourself that you are not the body. The body is going through the pain. Thank the body for going through this difficulty for you. Do you complain about pain? You need it for practicing enlightenment or it would not be happening. An in-body experience is necessary. The body unconditionally loves you so much it willingly surrenders to whatever process is ultimately in your best interest. You as divine love are beyond any limited state of existence.

We are all beyond the grasp of the temporal world, for eternal love is the supreme force of the universe. It is time to practice this truth. It is time to own this reality. It is time to make this the substance of all sharing with others. It is time to direct the film of life with a glorious vision of **Beyond Duality** confidence. It is time to dance and play the music of eternal love, and let go of the gyrations of the temporal world. It is time to make room for the perception that **the temporal world has no power over me**. Divine love and wisdom is the only power I recognize. That is my story and I'm sticking to it.

Notes – Month #6

Month #7

Remind yourself and others that our value, power and worth is not earned, it is inherent. We do not have divine love and God consciousness. We *are* divine love and God consciousness! We do not have value, power and worth. We *are* value, power and worth! It is inseparable from our very nature. When did Heaven ever have to justify or prove its value?

As soon as the story that we must earn our way to Heaven appears, the ego immediately shows up, whispering in our ear that we are *not good enough,* and that *we did not do it right.* We live, own and share our true value, power and worth by choosing to align our free will with showing up as a force of unconditional love right here, right now.

For the next month when you find yourself or others beating themselves up, stop! Offer the truth that no one can create a learning experience they do not need. We are all beyond this practice arena we call the planet Earth. We can all embrace our value, power and worth right now. We can all take it back from the ego and the temporal world as a quality that is earned and subject to change. We can all claim the victory. We can be value, power and worth in this present moment.

Notes – Month #7

Month #8

Practice your living, sharing, speaking and playing from the Heart not the head. **Enlightenment is the journey out of the head and into the Heart.** The Heart is where we all become as children and enter into the kingdom of Heaven. The Heart is, as the *Little Prince* reminds us, *"where we see what is essential, as it is invisible to the eye."* The Heart is where we are eternally young, truthful, optimistic, carefree and happy. The Heart is where we are going to practice making our eternal mailing address for the next month. Put your hand over your Heart, feel the beat, listen to the bio-rhythmic waves. The world is so loud and laden with sounds that it's important to practice rhythm renewal.

To practice living from the Heart, you will need to draw on the last seven months of practice. Living in the Heart happens when you remember you are divine love. Heartfelt sharing occurs when you remember everything unfolding here is governed by divine love and wisdom, sent to serve all of life. Make that the only power and story you recognize. A Heart-inspired life is a practice.

When you notice the ego talking to you, and of course, you will recognize it by its limiting voice, stop. Take a few deep breaths. Breathing deeply keeps you in the moment. Give your attention to Heaven. Let Heaven know you would like to let go of this load of mental shit. Don't be worried, Heaven is not offended by the word "shit". Heaven is beyond anything limited and would like you to be as well. Forget about language, practice freeing your mind instead.

Maintain the practice of ceasing to give attention to anything that sounds, tastes, looks or feels limiting. You may need more than one attempt toward self-satisfaction.

Continue to refocus your attention on the highest thing that you know. I suggest the Ultimate Truth that there is only the One. There is always infinite abundance. I do not have love. I am love! I am beyond the grasp of anything limiting or physical. We are not pretending these unwanted qualities away, we are creating fulfillment by willing our truth into existence.

Make time this month to let go of your usual routine. Allow for some spontaneous joy to possess you. There are some suggestions for ways to play in the section *Zen and the Art of Play* if you feel you need a jump-start from the Heart. I like to start my day with a few Bugs Bunny cartoons. That never fails in my world. List your favorite start the day play...

Most of all this practice involves never saying *didn't do it right, not good enough,* or *not enough time, love, money or opportunity* to yourself or another person. Be tolerant of yourself and others. Last time I looked America was still a free country. That means everyone here *does not have to think, look and feel the same as you to have value and to be respected.* Whatever happened to the saying, "I may not agree with what you say, but I would defend with my life your right to speak it"??? Let others go through what they need to in order to learn. After all, people cannot create a learning experience that they do not need. Let go of the hate-fest we all engage in. Accept others as the God consciousness in motion that they are, experiencing what they need in order to wake up and learn to become better people. **For one month do not judge or criticize yourself or another person.** Let go and let love be the senior intelligence that guides this month. Note your freedoms gained from judging refrains, potential time and energy saved and improved focus.

Notes – Month #8

Month #9

Practice seeing everyone, yourself included as God's creation. When you wake up in the morning and look at yourself in the mirror, wish well the God consciousness that you have been given. Treat yourself as you would God. Feed yourself the food you would offer God. If you would not offer God junk food, do not eat it. If you would not call God an ugly, stupid sack of dysfunctional shit, do not say that to yourself or others.

Would you ask God to work without any consideration for any relationship or activity that brings balance to life? Then do not engage in that or ask it of others. If you would be generous to God, then do so with others. If you see a homeless person on the street, wish them well in your Heart. See them as beyond the present limited physical condition. Require of yourself and others the same level of honesty and respect you would from God. Surrender the identical amount of patience and flexibility to others as you would to God. Imagine the Earth as populated by billions of walking God creatures. Make that your soul's sole story about others on the rock.

If you would like to practice a more advance version of this exercise, extend the God-ship to every animal and plant, as well as the Earth itself. Remember this month, that the family member, neighbor, coworker, fellow student that you have practiced disliking, is as much God as you are. Have fun with this one! Do not lose sight of the reality that in Heaven, everyone treats and sees everyone equally as God. So if Heaven is a place you would like to live in, I suggest you start practicing living there Now. One of the little helpful reminders I use is calling *everyone* I meet "Angel."

Breathing in a new point of view without bounds.

Notes – Month #9

Month #10

Practice gratitude for the whole of life, not just the parts you like. Not just that which makes you look and feel good, but the whole of life. Wake up every morning and acknowledge gratitude for everything in life. The spiritual truth is that no one can create an experience that they do not need. Therefore everything that occurs in our life is required in order to reach enlightenment. It therefore serves us immensely to be grateful for the whole of it. List something you were not grateful for and list it in a new light.

Being in a state of Heartfelt gratitude allows us as spiritual beings to receive the full benefit of the evolutionary process we are engaged in. Let's face it, if we've already gone through an experience then we have already paid whatever price we needed for it. After paying the price for life, we should at the very least orient ourselves to receive whatever maximum gift there is for going through it. You have paid the price now please receive the gift. Even if the lesson does not make sense to you at the time, continue the practice of gratitude and run gold through it (*see practice #8 in Zen and the Art of Play section*).

Practicing gratitude for the **whole of life** assists mind in neutrality and surrender as well. Neutrality and surrender begin to spread throughout the **whole of mind** when gratitude is practiced. By being grateful, mind is neutralizing the charges the ego has recreated about life. Practicing gratitude increases surrender; we cannot be grateful for the divine gifts we receive and be in a state of resistance, recreated by the ego, at the same time. **Create a new space in your Heart, the thanks tank.**

By giving attention to gratitude for the whole of life, we practice giving our attention to what lives in Heaven to the exclusion of anything limited. That is the name of the game here on the rock. By being grateful for the whole of life we begin to practice opening our minds and our perception. It is easier to recognize a gift that comes packaged in a challenging situation when you have practiced being grateful for everything. Without this practice of gratitude, mind will go to whatever limited stories and conclusions that it has practiced most. Limited stories and conclusions that look and sound like, *"Nothing I do ever turns out right." "Yes, once again disappointment and heartache have become my middle name."* The real problem with running negative charges like these is that due to the law of energy agreement, reality will go out of its way to continue to deliver experiences that match your stories. Trust me on this one – you would rather learn more from gratitude than from the pain and suffering of limitation.

The fastest way to increase the flow of what is life-sustaining is gratitude. If the body is in pain and experiencing great limitation, focus on being grateful for whatever health you do have. If the bank account looks anemic, focus on being grateful for the money you do have. If others have harmed you, focus an being grateful for the honest, loving, fair, supportive relationships that you do have. Whatever you want more of in your life, focus on being grateful for what you do have and the spiritual door will be opened for more to enter into your life through your Heart's door forevermore.

Aligning your Ruling Love with an attitude of gratitude is the fastest way to excel in spiritual development. Spend the next month working those gratitudinal spiritual muscles. Start in the morning when you wake up by being grateful for the rest and sleep that you did get. Being grateful for wherever you wake up. During the course of the day, should the attention wander off to reliving past unpleasant memories, use this as a reminder to be grateful for the whole of life. Be grateful for the people and relationships that have contributed in any way to the evolution of your soul. Because if you could reach enlightenment without the lessons they bring, they would not have been allowed to show up in your life. For everything and for everyone rejoice in a Heart-felt state of gratitude. Shout it out, tears too, celebrate your release, your peace . . .

Notes – Month #10

Month #11

Catch yourself in recreation patterns and stop immediately. Examine what unresolved stories and charges are involved in the perpetuation of the issue. Then focus on creating a new response to an old habit. As examined in *You Are What You Love,* all suffering originates from what you give your attention to. You are what you love and you love whatever you are giving your attention to. The ego lies to us distracting our attention from the truth that there is only the One. There is always infinite abundance. The ego loves to drag our attention to an unhappy place with the lies that you are *not good enough, did not do it right,* and/or with the *not enough (time, love, money, opportunity)* stories. **Your job is to take your mind back, to make up your Heart, not just your mind, and enjoy.**

This month is going to be spent catching the lies that mind has been recreating. You will recognize the lies by the limiting feelings and experiences they perpetuate and by the pervasiveness of the issues in your life. Your practice this month is to stop the inner dialog through the power of self-awareness. Know thyself! Then, because what you give your attention to creates your reality, focus on what you are wanting, not what you do not want. Practice creates a conscious response to an old unconscious pattern, thereby reprogramming that part of your memory.

Every time you catch a recreation story, instead of empowering it with more attention, you begin to erode its power and grip in your life. You did not practice worry and bad faith only once in your lifetime. So it makes sense you may have to practice dismantling it more than once as well. Just practicing catching and stopping the stories in your everyday life is an extremely potent practice. Don't let the lies slip under your inner truth radar.

The more you practice arresting the contamination in your mind, the better you will get at eliminating the ego's shit from your life and nervous system. The quicker you contain it, the less damage it can do and the faster you can get on with creating a new response. New responses worth cultivating are: *"I do not have love, I am love." "I do not earn value, power and worth, I own it." "I am beyond anything limited."* Time for the environmental mind cleanup crew, led by you!

The ultimate point of this practice is that you develop such a talent for it that your natural response is: To create a new response to the whole of life, without a single recreation pattern in mind. **You get that you are it – that's it!**

Notes – Month #11

Month #12

Practice owning and living the truth – that you and everyone else here does not have love, you are love unconditionally. **End the cycle of feeling and believing that love has to be earned or that it could be withheld.** Stop playing games with others on this issue. Withholding love is a form of spiritual abuse and it must stop if your life is to have any higher quality at all. When you become better practiced at seeing yourself as one with love, it will become easier to give it to yourself, as well as the more challenging people in your life. Who have you loved? Are you love/loved? Do you recognize love? What are your current love limits?

The more solidly aligned your mind is with the truth, that you do not have love, you are love, the more impossible it will be for the ego to interfere with this relationship. When Jesus announced that he and the Father are One, that was not the first time he ever practiced acknowledging and living that truth. Make this life your practice arena for oneness with that truth. When you catch yourself or others beating themselves up, **stop** the bad practice/ habits and speak the truth. Set your wave free instead! **Surf your love wave.**

When you find yourself disliking or criticizing another, maybe it is a politician, or political leader from another country, **STOP**. Remind yourself that they are love too! They are divine consciousness in motion reaching enlightenment the fastest most efficient manner possible. No one here has the power to do anything else. Ask yourself honestly how it benefits your life or the lives of others to run and maintain a story that other spiritual creatures are separate from love? How does that improve your life or the collective life of everyone on the rock?

Ask family members, friends, supportive relationships in your life, to assist you. Ask loved ones to point out where you are being self-critical or non-accepting or passing that buck on to others (they'll love this one!). Make a written contract with the close important people in your life that you individually and collectively will **NOT** use *did not do it right, not good enough* as well as not *enough time, love, money, opportunity* on yourself or any other living being.

There is great joy living a life of One Love. There is great power commanding the force of realized love. There is a fulfilling life governed by self-realization. The most celebrated awakened truth is *I do not have love, I am love!* If there is any truth in a Nike commercial then . . . just do it! Or in the higher reality . . . just *be* it! or "leave the love light on."

This year enjoy creative self-fulfillment! Celebrate this last month of mind/wave transformation! Obviously the growth, healing, enlightenment does not end with this exercise. This year was a helpful suggestion to create the foundation needed to support further unlim-

Notes – Month #12

ited self-realization. In the words of Mork from Ork . . . "Fly! Be free!"

Alternative Exercise or Month #13 (Lunar Calendar)

Should one of the earlier practices not speak to you, or if you feel some are close enough in intention that it feels repetitive, here is an alternative practice.

Practice seeing the red and green lights in your life. Practice acknowledging when you are experiencing a red or green light by letting the rest of your stories and attachments, to an outcome, simply fall away. If you apply for a job, or apartment, or college and you receive a letter or phone call informing you that you were not chosen, **STOP**. Take a deep breath. Remind yourself that all that has happened is that you have been given a red light. This allows you to free up your energy and shift the focus to finding the next green light.

"No is on backwards". – Argisle

No one can create a learning experience that they do not need. Heaven decides the movement of all things. How do you know when and where it would best serve you to direct your life force? By viewing the red and green lights given in your life. When you are driving across town in your car or riding on the bus, you do not interpret the changing of traffic lights as a personal rejection slip. You accept the light change as the agreed upon method that we are all subject to for determining where and when we all move forward. This is the best way to advance without causing injury to ourselves or others. So it is with the spiritual red and green lights revealed in our journey through life.

This month, practice recognizing a red light from a green light. You will practice having no stories or charges other than, stop now the light is red! Or move forward the light is green, until directed otherwise. This month you will practice not taking the movement of the red and green lights personally. This month, practice being directionally savvy. This month, practice saying to Heaven, "Thank you for the clarity of this red light. Now I know you wish me somewhere else. For there is an evolutionary gift for me in another area and without this red light how would I know to look elsewhere or with a green light to simply allow receptivity? Thank you!" This month, practice saying, "Thank you Heaven for this red/green light. Thank you for the gifts I receive. I will move forward or stop according to guidance, without an attachment to an outcome, without a thought or be-lief about what it all means or how it will all turn out" . . . talk about a risk-tak-er! A quest!

As human beings we can be so myopic about life. We have a tendency to become fixed and rigid in what we want and when we want it. It is only in hindsight that we realize, that it was actually a great thing end-ing up where we did, when we did. As we were unaware of what we would find until a future perspective offered us realization. Stop beating yourself up. Stop blam-ing others for disappointments. Be awake to the movement of the red and green lights given. Be neu-tral to the ego's commentary

Notes – Month #13

PLAYBOOK

Zen and the Art of Play

Reflect back on all you experienced as a child while playing. Consider what you prepared yourself for in the years to come by playing. Is there a single great painter who did not start out as a child throwing color on the wall, the furniture, themselves? Is there an extraordinary athlete who did not start out practicing as a child? Play has been humankind's perpetual groundwork for all advanced learning. Where and why do we lose touch with this fertile environment of magical imaginings and new beginnings?

> ❈ Now is the time to take back our divine potential as creative God creatures.
> ❈ Now is the time to recapture all that we have not developed and fulfilled to its higher promise.
> ❈ Now is the time to live the life we promised ourselves.
> ❈ Now is the time to play beyond a mortgaged life of limitation.

This section contains ideas, suggestions for playful exploration. Like the twelve-month practice these ideas are designed to be springboards that can easily be improved upon by tailoring them to your unique personality or developed deeper with your own creative touches. Feel free to enhance or modify any practice in this book, to what feels right to you Now.

> **This section also contains a lot of blank pages so you may be your own author:**
> ❈ Draw your responses to the practices.
> ❈ Journal ideas or responses that come to you.
> ❈ Make notes that you would like your future self, who looks back on this in 5 or 10 years, to read and remember. As always the sky is the limit. The great play wisdom I have learned, is that anything worth doing in a playful way, is worth overdoing.

It's extremely valuable to practice being creative that is the main idea with this playbook. **Healthy God consciousness creates something from nothing.** Starting a practice in the fine art of creativity is paramount to developing a practice by setting aside time for the sole purpose of cultivating your own special creative perspective. When we only practice recreating limitation over and over again, any attempt at creating a new response to an old issue, will immediately be experienced as overwhelming and feel frustrating as well. Isn't it comforting to know that the end to our suffering is only a creative moment away?

Enjoy playing around! Enjoy the moment! Enjoy making a monument to personal happiness! Enjoy ending recreation by learning to create a new response to life! Enjoy creating this section of the book as something that edifies your soul!

Practice #1

The new comic book is you! Invent a creative comic book version of yourself. The idea is to get rid of the old outdated perceptions of yourself as limited. Express yourself as endowed with superhuman qualities, the ones you are.

You can write a comic book version of yourself if writing appeals to you, or you can draw the new comic book you, or you can do both! A friend of mine told me that she held a constant fantasy about herself as the "incredible rubber woman." In her comic book version of self, she could reach around corners into other spaces without ever leaving her chair. She could extend her torso allowing her to change light bulbs in high ceilings while still standing on the floor. She could put away dishes in the back of tall cabinets without breaking stride while washing at the sink. She could retrieve the newspaper from the front lawn while still in bed. These details are only the smaller adventures of the incredible rubber woman.

I have always had a visual image of the comic book version of myself. My birthday is June 6th, which also happens to be D-day - the day the allies stormed the beaches of Normandy in World War II. So every year when I wake up on my birthday and turn on the television or radio, the first thing I hear is, "It's June 6th, D-day, the day all America mourns."

Well, let me tell you it's not very playful to hear repeatedly that your birthday is the day all America mourns. Unlike July 4th, which is the day all America blows its biggest, brightest and most sparkles in response to your birthday. As a result of this birthday association, my fantasy was that all the angel children in Heaven would be reading a comic book about my life, and the cover would show a playful version of me emerging from the ocean. The title of the comic book would read, "Armed only with a sense of humor she storms the spiritual beaches of Normandy!" Shatter the old you and long live the new comic book you! It's V-Day!!

Draw the new comic book YOU here!

Write the new comic book YOU story here!

Practice #2

Write a creative story or metaphor that reveals, depicts, or expresses a higher truth that is important to you. Let's begin with a story of my own:

Cast of Characters:

❋ **Quack** - a large black duck, representing the stuff we are here to get over.

❋ **The Purple Empress of the Imagination, Creativity** – the creative intelligence that resolves limitation by creating a new response to Quack.

❋ **Gift Boxes** - represent everything is as it should be.

❋ **Celestial Ship of Infinite Possibility** - represents the vehicle of enlightenment, the ever eternal present moment.

❋ **The Purple Dancing Dots of Bright Color** – represent remembering to give attention to the truth. Much like Hanzel and Gretel's bread crumbs which allowed them to remember how to return home.

The story begins like this:
The world was gathered together on the playing field of mind, when suddenly out of nowhere, Quack rushed off with the Purple Empress of Imagination. She left a trail of purple dancing dots of bright color behind her.

The Celestial Ship of Infinite Possibility filled with gift boxes came to the Empress' rescue, capturing Quack and thus foiling his intended kidnapping plan. Quack became immediately powerless when surrounded by the gift boxes. The Purple Empress of Imagination was at the helm navigating the ship to the land of Wholeness.

Once in the land of Wholeness complete memory of the truth is restored. The now embodied remembrance that everything that happens is actually Mind's creative journey to understand and know itself. Everything that we experience is actually God consciousness in motion reaching enlightenment the fastest most efficient way it can, because it does not have the power to do anything else. Everything is manifesting for the purpose of resolving our relationship with Quack.

Meanwhile back at the playing field of mind, the entire world was attempting to try to find the Purple Empress of Imagination, without following the dancing purple dots of bright color left behind. Following the purple dots of bright color would not only have led the world home, but they would also have made all relationships playful in the process of the journey.

Division, chaos and confusion broke out and the entire world scattered in different directions without any attention to the dancing purple dots of bright color.

Back at the land of Wholeness the Purple Empress of Imagination dissolved into pure empty space. Quack disintegrated into perfect nothingness.

Returning to the playing field of mind, the entire world recreated confusion and loss, totally forgetting its true purpose of following the purple dots of bright color. The Celestial Ship of Infinite Possibility and the gift boxes were not recognized by those lost in recreation. The remembrance that everything that occurs is mind working itself out became forgetfulness, loneliness and unhappiness.

Although Quack never regained his original form as a black duck, he did reappear invisibly in the perception of the world. His reappearance in perception manifested as the disease of duality, limiting and recreating forgetfulness of the truth.

Eventually the dancing purple dots of bright color could only be seen by those still seeking the Purple Empress of Imagination. Revealing themselves only to those of a pure Heart. Those who follow the dancing purple dots of bright color ultimately end their journey in the land of Wholeness. Those still focusing and following the now invisible voice of Quack remain recreating limitation and fear.

Recognition of the Purple Empress of Imagination occurs when attention is given to the remembrance of the truth. Everything that happens on the playing field of life is mind manifesting itself on the journey to the land of Wholeness. *The End.*

You now see the primary principals from *You Are What You Love,* expressed in this creative short story. Now it's your turn. Take a deep breath, whip out your finger paints, glow-in-the-dark pens, thread, glitter, and imagination.

Compose YOUR story here!

Practice #3

Read someone *The Little Prince* (see suggested reading list) or your favorite adventure fairytale. It can be just yourself, however sharing with others just increases the fun!

Practice #4

Make a list of the new higher truths you would like to agree to. For example:

Old Agreement - I justify giving my attention to worry, in response to the outer world.

New Agreement - When worry touches the nervous system, I use it to remind me to be grateful for the money, health, loving and honest relationships I do have. I no longer use worry to justify focusing on what I do not have.

List your new agreements here!

Practice #5

In your next bath experience, if you have a bathtub, get some toys and play like you did when you were a kid. Go wild! Give yourself permission to expand beyond the ubiquitous rubber ducky motif. Play like it was the last bath you were ever going to take – bubbles, salts, essential oils and all!

Practice #6

Make a list of your favorite happy songs, or songs that have a special meaning or significance for you. Make your own customized tape or CD to play when you need uplifting. I have a tape with Jimi Hendrix playing *Little Wing* and *Spanish Castle Magic*, The Beatles' *Revolution*, and Louis Armstrong and Duke Ellington performing *It Don't mean A Thing (If It Ain't Got That Swing)*. I threw in some Lena Horn singing *It's Love* and Aretha Franklin doing *Rock Steady*. Then topped it off, like whipped cream with The Grateful Dead's *Uncle John's Band* and *Saint of Circumstance*. Pick whatever moves your Soul and then move to it! *Whistle While You Work* and *Love Is A Dream Your Heart Makes* are suggested!

List your happy songs here!

Practice #7

Clear out the clutter in your life. Make a day of it. Go through as much or as little clutter as you want in your creative adventure. Maybe it is just a closet or a drawer. Maybe it is the entire garage. You pick the mountain you want to climb. Then throw out the clutter, recycling or giving it away, whenever possible to someone who could benefit from it. From the looks of it, the fab five on the television program *Queer Eye For The Straight Guy* appear to make a great sport out of throwing out the old and preparing for the new. Enjoy identifying with the eternal, not the temporal. Celebrate living freely and not being owned by your possessions. Have fun with clearing out your inner space by emptying the outer … out out!

When the space has been cleared of past things that are no longer useful in the present moment, then do a creative imagin- ing. Imagine the new space being filled with awakened love. Give the imagined incom- ing love a color if you like. See a scale in your mind's eye that goes from zero to one hun- dred. Keep filling the space in your imag- ining with the qual- ity you want until the scale goes to one hundred. Claim the space for love, compassion, and happiness. What- ever floats your boat and rocks your world! Clutter free is confu- sion free and that is an infinitely more play- ful state of mind.

Practice #8

In psychic school (yes, there is such a thing), we were taught a very fun practice known as "running gold." The idea is as follows: because you do not have consciousness you are consciousness, whatever you give your attention to has great power. My Qi Gong teacher used to say, *"Wherever you place your awareness is where the energy goes."* Building on these principles, if you imagine a gold light or a gold energy running somewhere, gold energy will go there. In Divine Correspondence gold represents the highest, the best, the most refined and precious of what we know. "Go" are the first two letters of "gold!"

Imagine running gold through your body, the energy goes there, and you practice filling your body with the best that you know now. You can run gold through your house, dorm room, workplace, or car. I run gold through my pets, through my food, my clothes, a pool before swimming, a plane before flying. I run gold through a dream I remember. Run gold through a calendar. After all, time only exists in the imagination as a mental concept. Run gold anywhere, anytime you want! It costs you nothing but your focused self and helps to integrate the highest wisdom you know, in a golden, playful way.

Always wanted more gold in your life but thought you could not afford it? Well, play with the only gold that you do take with you, now in this moment, free of taxes, tariffs and exchange rates. If this sounds a little too far out in la la land for you, please attempt a moment of open mindedness. After you have run gold for some time see if it helps you feel better. If your ego tells you that feeling better is all in your "head," remind yourself that is where all of life takes place anyhow.

Practice #9

This next practice is a modified version of a shamanic soul retrieval. Imagine a part of yourself that you feel has gotten lost or damaged along life's journey. After being lied to and cheated on you feel you have lost your trusting nature, or possibly you feel you have had your inner child damaged by abuse or relentless adult responsibilities. Perhaps you feel your natural playfulness and imagination have been dulled by too much right brain activity, and you would like your parts back. Whatever it is, get in touch with some aspect of your soul that you feel needs to be enlivened. Get a sense for what is missing and then invite it back. Either in an inner dialog, or in the enclosed blank pages, communicate with that part of mind and ask it to return. Let this part of mind know why you miss it - what you are willing to do to protect it in the future so that your life is now a safe haven for its return.

Let the lost or damaged quality talk with you. Let it tell you what it needs. Let it speak to your Heart. Most importantly let the relationship grow into an attitude of gratitude for the whole of life and its numerous experiences. Sing a few choruses of "I can't create a learning experience I do not need." Invite your mind back and then set it free with your Heart.

Let the lost you communicate here!

Practice #10

Imagine the world you want to live in, then practice living in it. If you want to live in a world where you are given help when you ask for it, create that world now. Give help to others when they ask for it. If you want to live in a world where everyone has a positive loving attitude, choose it. I cannot tell you how many times strangers, like cashiers at a store or other random people standing in a line with me, will ask me, *"Are you always like this? Are you always so positive and playful?"* My response is always the same, *"Out of all the things that happen today, my attitude and my nose may be the only things I get to pick. So I pick well and wisely."* The truth is I'm creating the world I want to live in. And my world is fun, very, very fun!

If you want to live in a worry-free world, do not build a monument to worry with your attention. Live in a world where your motto is, *"There is only the One. There is always infinite abundance."* If you want to live in a beautiful world, add beauty to your world. If you find yourself complaining about life on the rock, stop! Put your shoulder to the karmic wheel that you most want to support.

And let the transformation begin!

Sing a few rounds of, "*I am what I love and I love what-ever I give my attention to. Whatever I love is also going to determine where I live, as I do not exist separate from what I love.*" Got a nice rhythm to it, doesn't it? Remind your-self, "*I got music, I got rhythm, I am love. Who could ask for anything more?*"

Practice #11

Practice making fun of your fears and letting go of all limitation. We are so good at being fearful and limited because we practice it everyday. Have some fun reversing that unpleasant habit. Every time you become aware of a fear or a limited story, tell the issue, "I'm not taking you seriously today." Practice what Glenda the Good Witch of the North does in response to the Wicked Witch of the West, in the Wizard of Oz. Glenda remains firmly in the present moment. She looks the Wicked Witch in the eye and says, *"Be gone, before someone drops a house on you!"* Then wave your inner magic wand of remembrance that you do not have love you are love, and that everything here on the rock is working for your liberation or it would not be allowed to exist.

Wear an immortal Teflon attitude! Let the fear and the limited slide right off! As the eternally talented actor James Dean used to say, "Dream as if you'll live forever. Live as if you'll die today." Puts things right in perspective, don't it?

I am fond of the deathbed test. I do it all the time. I constantly ask myself, "On my deathbed will this be important to me?" If the answer is "yes" I give it the proper due. If the answer is "no" I drop it and move on.

Make a pledge to yourself, *"Today I am going to practice living a fearless life. Today I will live in a manner that honors and remembers the unlimited, and the eternal."* Don't get me wrong, you may not find yourself completely enlightened just because you made an inner pledge, but practice does make perfect.

The idea here is that you are eternal God consciousness. You are greater than the fears and the limitations you have come here to leave behind. You can practice a fun and playful way to enliven the eternal over the temporal. You can update the song *I Got The Power* to ***I am The Power!***

Practice #12

Remind the important relationships in your life that you love and value their presence, in your existence here on the rock. Bringing attention to the relationships in your lives that are irreplaceable will always enhance your present moment. When my significant other and I sit down to a meal, we always clink our glasses together and toast to the gift of another wonderful day with the love of our life.

I have a friend Sarah who always tells me how much she loves and values my presence in her life, whenever I say something that makes her laugh. I have another dear friend Pela who always starts out every phone conversation with an affirmation of gratitude for our connection. These perspective finders are the precious jewels and gleaming gold of our lives. Do not let your life slip by without consciously mining for the best blessed.

On his television show, Dr. Phil, the relationship expert, will often share with the audience his nightly ritual with his two sons. In this tradition, Dr. Phil says he asks his boys how did he get so lucky as to have the best boys in the world. I don't know about you, but after hearing about that nocturnal tradition, I would have traded in my entire childhood for one day with Dr. Phil as my Dad.

I have given some great examples here of how to honestly, in a Heartfelt manner, acknowledge the meaningful people in your lives. You can forge your own signature, custom, tailor made, Heartfelt sharing that is as unique as you and your relationships are. Usually it is as simple as dropping into your Heart and letting your feelings express themselves fully and honestly. The words will find you, if you make yourself available. At first it may seem awkward if you have not established a pattern of open communication, but do not let that stop you. It is easy to become relaxed and confident with a habit or choice or practice that feeds the soul.

Ask yourself, *"On my deathbed will it be important that the people who have meant the most to me know that I loved and treasured our time together?"* If the answer is *"yes,"* give it the proper due in your life. The time is now. If you are reading this, then it is not too late. Be the relationship you always wanted. Speak the truth you always wanted to hear. In the words of Dr. Phil, *"Be a soft place to land for those you love."* In the words of Madonna, *"Express yourself."* In the wisdom of Jesus, *"Love others as I have loved you."* But most importantly find the words within yourself that yearn to be shared and then give those magical, golden words life.

Practice #13

Take the playful times of your life back! Is there something you used to love to cook or bake, but have forsaken it for the microwave and frozen food section? Take it back! Is there a creative form of expression such as drawing or painting or writing that you have put on the back burner for so long it is now growing mold? Take it back! Is there a musical instrument gathering dust in some corner of your life? Take it back! Is there a jewelry making or beading talent stagnating in your day to day existence? Take it back! Is there a favorite walk or meaningful poem?

Go to you window, open it up and shout "I'm as creative as Heaven and I'm going to take it back!" If you are a film fan you will recognize that last statement as a bastardized line from the movie *Network*. This is one of my favorite films. I will not let life go by without watching that film when I can find it. The great film director Frank Capra is one of my heroes. I own many of his films, because I will not let the enjoyment of these fine expressions of art wither and die on the vine of *"not enough time."* **If it feeds your soul, take it back!**

If you come alive working with wood, make the time to construct something. If you love gardening, plant something. If you have the best memories of sharing a creative activity with a loved one, find the opportunity to do it! You can play, cook, build, garden, sew, write, paint, draw or share stories. Whatever it is that enriches your soul . . . take it back!

You are never to old to play and create. I love to color in coloring books, just as I did when I was five. When I watch television at night I have all my colored pens and pencils spread around me. I spend hours coloring in books. My favorite is *Tara's Coloring Book* by Wisdom Publications (ISBN #0-86171-002-9). This is not your ordinary coloring book. This is a very complex coloring book. It contains very detailed pictures of Buddhist Deities. I showed a friend of mine the coloring book recently, their jaw dropped and they said, *"You colored these in? These are amazing!"* I just laughed and said *"Yeah. My past lives as Buddhist monks and nuns are showing up, in colorful style – huh!"*

Valuing creativity is the point. **Gaining the mastery of creating something from nothing is the purpose.** Manifesting enlightenment from space is the ultimate in creativity. Every creative venture strengthens this ultimate creative movement. So sign up for the swing dance class you have always wanted to take. Learn to make that stained glass project you have always wanted to do. These experiences are steps in awakening. These creative practices are God consciousness reaching enlightenment the fastest most efficient way it can. As God consciousness we do not have the power to do anything else. Heal the Earth playfully!

Practice #14

Practice slowing your life down. The following suggestions may at first incite the fear of God in you, but please breath deeply and relax into the possibility. Just let these suggestions wash over your mind and nervous system.

Try these suggestions for a day, or longer. If you dare, make your own list.

❋ Try turning off your cell phone, the TV, be quiet.

❋ Try driving the speed limit.

❋ Leave the house without everything being perfect.

❋ If your partner did not fold the towels and/or sheets absolutely correctly, let it go.

Ask yourself on your deathbed, will this be important to me? If the answer is *"yes,"* give it the appropriate due. If the answer is *"no,"* let it go. Make your present moment motto *"I do my best and let the rest go."* Value slowing down your life versus doing. Value appreciating this moment over valuing *"what did I get done."* Value joy and happiness rather than productivity. Remember you lived before you had a cell phone and the world did not come to an end. Remember what is really important to you and not what the ego dictates out of habit. Creating a mindset where there is enough time, love, money and opportunity - this is your next creativity challenge. Ready, set, gold!

Practice #15

Fun, for the sake of fun! Get together with friends and play baseball, or football, or cards, or my favorite game - strip monopoly. Every time you pass GO, you collect $200.00, take a shot of whiskey and take off an article of clothing! Trust me, with strip monopoly capitalism goes out the window rather rapidly. It does not matter what you play. Any game is good to practice playing for the sake of playing. Unfortunately much of play has become contaminated by competition. Playing for the sake of playing takes all the hard feelings out of game playing. Competition invites *better than* and *less than* into the mind. The purpose of play is to create a new response to that old tiresome story and make space for more shared joy.

Another way to play for the sake of playing is to have a playgroup. There are groups that get together to discuss reading the latest books. Instead you can create a group that explores venues for play, as well as the effects upon one's life when engaged in creative play. Have a creative swap party. For example, I invent different play excursions with my friends. We have what I call "gluing shit to your shoes day." My lady friends get together and we all glue rhinestones, plastic doo-dads and artificial flowers, etc. to a pair of sandals or flip-flops. In my community there is a restaurant that has a fortuneteller on Friday evenings. So my friends and I make reservations for fortune telling Friday, and we all play at the restaurant. We also like to get together for the Sunday brunch tradition. We pick some fun place to go. We spend Sunday afternoon visiting and catching up in each other's lives, or storytelling over Sunday brunch.

One of my absolute favorite play excursions is to the town of Tombstone, Arizona. Once a year my friends join me in a three day journey to Tombstone. We stay at my favorite Bed and Breakfast, *The Buford House,* run by Ruth and Richard, they are an incredibly fun couple who spoil you with their fabulous breakfast! The town of Tombstone holds a Wild West theme event nearly every month of the year. Most of the people who attend, dress in 1880's period costumes. My friends and I always dress up as saloon girls. We like to walk up to the men dressed like Wyatt Earp, poke them in the chest with our fingers and say, *"Just try to run women like us out of town . . . just try!"* The great thing about Tombstone is that everyone is playing dress up! And you thought the memory of invading your parents clothes closet was fun. This is that same fun only logarithmically increased and taken to an adult level of accessorizing and being street-legal!

Creating play for the sake of play can be manifested when we take/make the time to play. Take a day off once a week or once a month as a mental health day and play. A balanced life is essential in living a healthy life. As Stephen King has already pointed out in horrific detail, *"All work and no play, makes Jack a dull boy."* If you have a dog, take your dog out to the beach, the park, whatever. Let your dog teach you how to play, again. Remember you are never too old to play or have fun.

It does not matter if it is miniature golfing, boating, having a picnic or a barbecue. Fun is what you make of it. **If your life has no fun, you have no life.** A life without play, is a life not worth living. Be your own fun guru! Enlighten your day with play! On your deathbed will it have been important to you that you played to the best of your ability, or will you feel you should have worked and labored more? Whichever one it is, give it the appropriate due.

Personally, I am transforming beyond the life bardo, the death bardo and I am headed straight for the play bardo . . . catch me if you can!

Surrendering to love, to eternal consciousness is like one big free-fall
through life.

Also Available from the Author

The companion book to the
You Are What You Love Playbook:
You Are What You Love

Excerpts from:
You Are What You Love Book
on CD

Available at:
www.purplehazepress.com
www.youarewhatyoulove.com

You can also contact Vaishali by going to either website
and clicking on contact us.